S0-AHN-901

HEADQUARTERS SPECIAL TROOPS
Office of the Catholic Chaplain
ARO 403, New York, New York

14-27

THE BIBLE IN THE CHURCH

CANTERBURY BOOKS

THE BIBLE
IN THE CHURCH

59728

by

BRUCE VAWTER, C.M.

BS587
.V29B

BS 587 .V29b · ST. JOSEPH'S UNIVERSITY · STX

The Bible in the church.

3 9353 00005 3148

SHEED AND WARD · NEW YORK

© Sheed & Ward, Inc., 1959

Library of Congress Catalog Card No. 59–6396

Imprimi Potest: James W. Stakelum, C.M.
Superior provincialis
August 20, 1958

Nihil Obstat: Rt. Rev. Matthew P. Stapleton, S.T.D., S.S.L.
Diocesan Censor Deputatus

Imprimatur: ✠ Richard Cardinal Cushing
Archbishop of Boston

November 21, 1958

Manufactured in the United States of America

To the Vincentian Fathers of the faculty of
Saint Mary's College
Strawberry Hill
Twickenham, Middlesex

Contents

Foreword

This little book is intended as a brief explanation
of the role played by the Bible in the life of the
Catholic Church. Conscious of the somewhat different role in which the Bible has been cast in the
English-speaking world through generations of
"Bible religion," the author has found it necessary
to speak as often of what the Bible is not as of
what it is. He has done so only with the intention
of making the Catholic position more understandable, as he hopes, to the non-Catholic as well as
the Catholic. It is for the latter, however, that the
book is chiefly intended, who living in a largely
Protestant society may find it helpful to be re-
minded of the history of the Bible in the Church
and of what is implied in the claim that the Bible
is a Catholic book.

CHAPTER 1

Who Closed the Open Bible?

One does not, I should think, ordinarily turn to the *Canterbury Tales* for instruction in the Bible. Still, there is some to be found there, if only to this extent, that the *Tales* show our fellow pilgrims, a motley of the chosen and the damned as in every age of the Church, those to whom the Bible was a customary book. Far more customary, when we come to think of it, than in our own highly literate times. On the way to Canterbury, scriptural deeds and sayings and biblical figures of speech and of chronicle appear and reappear casually on strange and unlikely lips—strange and unlikely, that is to say, were the pilgrims our contemporaries, as they otherwise might be in so many ways.

Frequent allusions to the Old and New Testaments are, of course, altogether in character in the nun's priest's tale, and we are not too sur-

prised to find the same thing in the story of
Melibeus. But it would hardly occur to one of the
present-day much-married sisters of the wife of
Bath, that eternal Englishwoman, to frame her
apologia by twisting the scriptural saws still cited
against her by pious souls:

> What rekketh me, thogh folk seye vileinye
> Of shrewed Lameth and his bigamye?
> I woot wel Abraham was an holy man,
> And Jacob eek, as ferforth as I can;
> And ech of hem hadde wyves mo than two;
> And many another holy man also.

Neither can we easily imagine one of our nowadays merchants telling the tale in which Proserpine retorts the canard of the "Solomon" of
Ecclesiastes, who in his travels had found no
good woman:

What make ye so muche of Salomon?
What though he made a temple, goddes hous?
What though he were riche and glorious?
So made he eek a temple of false goddis,
How mighte he do a thing that more forbode is?
Pardee, as faire as ye his name emplastre,

He was a lechour and an ydolastre;
And in his elde he verray god forsook.
And if that god ne hadde, as seith the book,
Y-spared him for his fadres sake, he sholde
Have lost his regne rather than he wolde.

It is not to the point that we should probably
be as much surprised to find our merchant knowl-
edgeable of Proserpine as of the Book of Kings.
The point is that those of whom and for whom
Chaucer wrote his poetry were unassumingly and
as a matter of course familiar with the Bible as a
text of living literature.

That Chaucer has, indeed, taken his figures
from life and, in this as in other respects, has ac-
curately mirrored an England that really existed
can be verified by anyone who will take the time
to read the scholarly study which Dr. Beryl
Smalley has made of the use of the Bible in the
Middle Ages.[1] Although her research is concerned
chiefly with the knowledge of the Bible evidenced
by the clergy rather than by layfolk, nevertheless
she incidentally shows that the laity's acquaintance with the Scriptures was general and fairly
wide.

[1] *The Study of the Bible in the Middle Ages,* 2d ed. (Oxford: Basil Blackwell, 1952).

This lay knowledge of Scripture in the Middle Ages was largely second-hand, it is true, even as the evidence in the *Canterbury Tales* would usually suggest. Reading was almost exclusively a clerical accomplishment. But even the humblest layman had open to him a variety of ways by which he could become familiar with the Bible's contents, not the least of which were the colleagues of the gentle parson, whom Chaucer also took from life:

> A good man was ther of religioun,
> And was a povre Persoun of a toun;
> But riche he was of holy thoght and werk.
> He was also a lerned man, a clerk,
> That Cristes gospel trewly wolde preche;
> His parisshens devoutly wolde he teche.

And if the parson's "tale" is a sample of this teaching, we are afforded by his moral treatise which he has so liberally salted with Scripture, and by the extraordinary patience and good will with which the pilgrims listened to it, another proof of the different sort of men we now are, who are inclined to find the same experience more than a little tedious.

If the Bible was known to the general public largely by word of mouth and indirectly, it was of first-hand acquaintance to those professionally devoted to the works of religion. Dr. Smalley writes:

> Following Cassian the founders of western monasticism incorporated *lectio divina* or *lectio sacra* into their rules. St. Benedict allotted two hours on weekdays, three in Lent, to private reading; on Sundays it replaced manual work. The books of the Bible were to be distributed to the brothers for reading during Lent. In his rule for nuns St. Caesarius of Arles ordered two hours of private reading a day, and reading aloud during spinning. Even when about their other work, the nuns were "always to ruminate something from Holy Scripture." In addition to reading at meal times the religious would hear the lessons read out in church; and at the eight daily offices prescribed by St. Benedict they recited the whole Psalter each week.[2]

Nor was this study always merely pious and untutored. The Middle Ages were hardly critical in the matter of religion as a rule, but they were far more critical than some of us today realize. The

[2] *Op. cit.*, p. 29.

monks who copied out the sacred texts by hand
from generation to generation and so preserved
them until the age of printing, who in the process
of this manuscript tradition made the Bible the
best documented of all the works of antiquity,
were not invariably ignorant of the scientific side
of the work they were doing. Anyone who has seen
a mediaeval manuscript Bible cannot fail to agree
that for its scribe it must have been a labor of love.
Sometimes it was also a labor of scholarship. For

> already the manuscripts of the Bible cor-
> rected by Alcuin's contemporary, Theodulf,
> bishop of Orleans, show traces of compari-
> son with the Hebrew text. Remigius has
> shown that such comparisons were not ex-
> ceptional. There were many attempts by
> scholars to learn at least the Hebrew alpha-
> bet. An Irishman of the ninth century, per-
> haps Sedulius Scotus, wrote a treatise in the
> form of a letter on the translation of the
> Psalter from Greek into Latin and on its tex-
> tual emendation. The writer had a good
> knowledge of Greek.[3]

Admittedly, these were not every-day occurrences. Nevertheless, they did happen. Perhaps

[3] *Ibid.*, p. 43.

what is most interesting of all to a modern scholar
is a manuscript reproduced in photograph by Dr.
Smalley, of a Hebrew Psalter glossed by a thir-
teenth-century friar who appears to have been the
pupil of Jewish teachers. He has noted in a margin
that the sacred and unuttered name of God, called
the *tetragrammaton* from its four Hebrew con-
sonants *YHWH* (and usually given as "LORD" in
our English Bibles), was to have the pronuncia-
tion *Iahave*. He was, as it is now agreed, absolutely
correct. What makes it surprising is that he knew
more than those who followed him in the Renaissance and Reformation, who popularized the impossible "Jehovah."

What all this has been leading to is the suggestion that ignorance of or indifference to the Bible
is not historically one of the notes of Catholicity,
contrary impressions notwithstanding. The contemporary of Chaucer who wrote the *Imitation of
Christ* and who called Holy Writ and the Eucharist
the light and life of his spiritual existence voiced
the real belief of his age. Not always with the in-
struments of study that are available to us after
centuries of trial-and-error and some very lucky
discoveries, and often making mistakes we no
longer have to make, our Catholic ancestors did,

despite all, indeed read the Bible and treasure that reading.

Because of some peculiarities of history, it is unfortunately necessary to issue special reassurances on this point to those for whom Bible-reading is to all practical purposes synonymous with the story of the English Bible. With other language groups the story is not quite the same. But who does not know that the first translation of the Bible into English was the work of John Wycliffe, a poor preacher who for his pains incurred the excommunication of the Catholic Church? Who has not seen the picture that was once standard in all works of Victorian piety, of the devout family gathered about a great volume, keeping a wary eye on the windows and door while the father read aloud, and in peril of the lives of all, the Bible of the same John Wycliffe—another of Chaucer's contemporaries! It is from this picture, rather than from the *Canterbury Tales*—for Wycliffe's followers did not go on pilgrimages—that the average English-speaking Protestant has derived his ideas about the Catholic Church's habitual attitude towards the reading of the Bible by the laity.

And, to be sure, the picture has its basis in fact, for such were the orders of the synod of Oxford held under Archbishop Arundel in 1408:

We therefore decree and order that no one
shall in the future by his own authority translate the text of Sacred Scripture into the
English or any other language, whether in the
form of a book, a booklet, or a pamphlet.
Neither shall anyone read any such book,
booklet, or pamphlet, either as recently composed by the said John Wycliffe or by anyone
else, or which may be composed in the future—neither in whole nor in part, neither
publicly nor privately, under penalty of a
major excommunication—until such time as
the translation has been approved by the
bishop of the diocese or, should such be the
case, by a provincial council. Those acting
contrarily will be punished as promoters
alike of heresy and error.

The language of this text is uncompromising
enough, and it is fairly typical of many decrees
that were issued by ecclesiastical authority in connection with vernacular translations of the Bible.
But like any other document it can be understood
only in the framework of its historical context. On
the one hand it reflects an attitude of the Church
that was present from the beginning and is still

operative, that is therefore timeless; but it also contains that which would not make sense outside fifteenth-century England.

What the English bishops of the synod of Oxford denounced was not the translation of the Bible into the vernacular, but translations undertaken by purely private authority without the approval of the Church. This was a policy that derives from the very origins of the Church and that remains unchanged today. The Catholic Church did then and does now regard the Bible as her own business. She considers herself to stand in relation to the Bible somewhat in the manner of a modern publisher with regard to a book of which he holds the copyright. However arrogant or unhistorical a non-Catholic may deem this position to be; he must bear it in mind if he would honestly understand much of what the Church has done in connection with the Bible.

The copyright on the present book is supported by the laws and conventions of various countries. Granting the improbability that anyone would want to reprint it, he could do so only at the risk of the penalties of law wherever the copyright is legally implemented. But where no copyright agreement exists among nations, "pirated" editions can be readily brought out, as was done in

America with British books in the last century, and as I believe can be done now in Soviet Russia with the books of Western countries. The Catholic Church is recognized today as a public and legislative society only by her own members, not by any nation, except within some very sharply defined limits in countries where there is a concordat with the Holy See. In the England of John Wycliffe theoretically it was otherwise, but in practice the Church's coercive power to enforce her laws was restricted to the spiritual penalties she could impose on those who admitted her right. The excommunication which she attached to the dissemination of Wycliffe's Bible was her way of asserting her "copyright."

It is one of the unfortunate circumstances of history, as far as English readers of the Bible are concerned, that only a relatively short time before the appearance of Wycliffe's Bible the Church felt it necessary to enforce her copyright. The editors of the Roman *Index Librorum Prohibitorum* itself state in their introduction that "during the first twelve centuries the reading of Sacred Scripture was quite customary with Christians . . . nor did ecclesiastical authority ever intervene to prohibit it." This statement is fully confirmed by the facts. The explanation there given of the Church's practice with regard to vernacular Bibles is a sane and reasonable one which will be of considerable interest even to those whose viewpoint on the subject may be quite different, and it merits being understood more widely than is commonly the case.

The "first twelve centuries" is no exaggeration. The Bible, after all, was originally written in the language of the people. (The vulgar Greek of the New Testament offended the eyes and ears of the Renaissance scholars.) When the New Testament was composed, Greek was at least the second language of anyone who could read or write at all. The Old Testament had long been available in Greek to those—who now included most Jews themselves—for whom Hebrew was a foreign language. When Greek was supplanted by Latin as the common language of the West, Bibles in Latin speedily followed. St. Jerome's famous Vulgate began not as a new translation but as an attempt to revise and edit previously existing Latin versions. It remained the Bible of Western Christendom for a thousand years. The edition which came from the press of Johannes Gutenberg around 1452 was the first book—and thus, of course, the first Bible —ever to be printed.

The Latin-*versus*-the-vernacular controversy has obscured the truth that the Bible in Latin be-

gan as a people's Bible. Just as millions of very
ordinary people in Italy, Holland, and other Eu-
ropean countries are today in a sense bilingual,
knowing both the national language and the local
dialect (which is sometimes a different tongue altogether), so for a very long time throughout much
of Europe Latin was spoken along with the beginnings of the vernaculars, which were themselves
dialects with wide local variations. Even when
Latin had definitely ceased to be the language of
the people, it remained the language of the literate;
it was long before the vernaculars became more
than what most of the modern dialects are, languages that are spoken but not written. The future
of Italian was not secure until Dante assured the
permanence and dominance of the Tuscan dialect
in which he wrote. *The Song of Roland* did much
the same for the *langue d'oïl*. In England the development of a national language was further complicated by the Norman conquest, which to a certain extent forced the process to begin all over
again. In the early tenth century the "English
Bible" would have run like this, citing Psalm 1,
1–2 from the so-called *Paris Psalter:*

Eadig by se wer the ne gaedh on ge theaht
unrihtwisra, ne on tham wege ne stent syn-

fulra, ne on heora wolbaerendum setle ne
sitt. Ac his willa bydh on Godes ae, and ymb
his ae bydh smeagende daeges and nihtes.

Within another century this language, which in
any case had never been that of all England, was
becoming as foreign to the contemporary English-
man as it is to us today.

In view of the slow development and the un-
certainty of the vernaculars, it is not surprising
that there were relatively few translations of the
Bible into obscure and now forgotten Gallic or
British dialects, though we have every reason to
believe that the full number of translations made
was far larger than those about which we actually
know. We know that a part of the Bible at least
existed as early as the seventh century in a Saxon
paraphrase attributed to Caedmon. The Venerable
Bede in the eighth century also translated a considerable part of the Bible into the northern English tongue. Certainly at the time of the Norman
conquest at least the Gospels and the Psalter had
been put into Anglo-Saxon. A great deal more of
such activity can be suspected, but unfortunately
not proved.

Another factor of which we must remind ourselves is that the invention of printing caused an intellectual and literary revolution the like of which has not been seen since in our world. Whereas at the beginning of the fifteenth century every book in existence was the result of laborious copying by hand, which made its cost simply out of the reach of all but the very wealthy, by the end of the same century presses were at work everywhere in Europe which could produce a thousand or two thousand copies of a book as easily as a single copy. The invention of printing coincided almost exactly with the beginning of the Protestant Reformation. It is for this reason also, therefore, to be expected that so many of the early vernacular Bibles should be Protestant in inspiration, for Protestantism had motives not shared by Catholicism that encouraged the wide dissemination of the Bible in the vernacular, and the means for this had never before been so ideal. But for printing, post-Reformation Bibles would be rarer today, even if not as rare as those dating from before the Reformation. The production of a manuscript Bible might take a careful scribe the better part of his lifetime, and the number of careful scribes was always limited.

And withal, it was not Protestantism that first gave the vernacular Bible to the laity. In the library of the provincial mother house of my religious community in Missouri is a large German Bible with interesting woodcut illustrations that was published in 1483, the year of Martin Luther's birth. I have encountered those who could never conceive that such a thing could exist, whose notion of the Reformation is that Luther discovered the Bible as a long forgotten, cobwebby tome, which revealed to his startled eyes the doctrine of justification by faith, and which he forthwith translated that all the people might find the same. I am aware that educated Protestants know better than this, yet some vestiges of this *legenda aurea* still linger even in their thinking.

As a matter of fact, at least sixteen translations of the complete Bible into German had already appeared before Luther's, all of them with ecclesiastical approval. To a greater or less degree, the story was the same in most of the other countries of Europe.

In the manuscript era a development of vernacular versions similar to that in England occurred also in the other countries of western Europe. Early French activity seems to have culminated in a Norman-French Bible made at the University of Paris and used in northern France around 1250. In Germany early fragmentary translation is exemplified by the Monsee fragment of Matthew, by a gospel harmony, and by an old Saxon poem *Heiland* ("Savior"), of the ninth century. Translations multiplied so rapidly that before the time of Luther about fifty complete German editions had been produced! In most of the Western countries, owing doubtless to the earlier impact of the Reformation, printed editions of the Scriptures appeared sooner than in England. Beginning with the Strasbourg German Bible of Mentel in 1466, there were eighteen printings in German before the important Luther New Testament of 1522 and Bible of 1534. In French the first printing, a New Testament, occurred about 1478 at Lyons, and the complete Bible appeared in 1487. Even before this, the Italians (1471) and Dutch (1477) had their Bible in the printed vernacular. Swedish, Bohemian, Slavonic, Russian, and Danish printing in whole or in part preceded English.[4]

---

[4] Allen Wikgren, article "The English Bible," in *The Interpreter's Bible*, Vol. I, p. 86. Copyright 1952 by Pierce & Smith. By permission of Abingdon Press.

In this connection I have deliberately cited a
Protestant rather than a Catholic scholar, though
the facts are for anyone to verify. In his statement
I think we can safely reject at least as an adequate
explanation his suggestion that the earlier biblical
activity of the Continent was "doubtless" due to
the earlier impact of the Reformation—here are
the traces of the *legenda aurea* mentioned above.
For in the main he is referring to versions that were
produced under solidly Catholic auspices, and he
includes countries where the Reformation never
made any impact at any time. Protestant authors
sometimes show an understandable tendency to
attribute to the Reformation whatever good things
happened after it. The same author, after noting
the early essays in England towards a vernacular
Bible which we have seen above, goes on to say
that

> a complete translation, however, is unknown
> in this Anglo-Saxon period. No real popular
> demand for such a production existed since
> few people could read, and manuscripts were
> too expensive for the average person to buy.
> A Bible for laymen was also unthinkable in
> the medieval church, which saw in the wide
> use of the Bible a threat to unity and to ec-

clesiastical control over the interpretation of the text, as well as a profanation of the Scriptures through such rough dialects as the Anglo-Saxon. Yet much of the biblical contents was made known through ritual, art, religious drama, and Bible picture books, the so-called *Biblia pauperum* or "Bibles of the poor."[5]

Here I am sure there is no justification, at least in any general sense, for the third sentence, which in fact is belied by the existence of *any* vernacular version whatever. If, as is an admitted fact, the Gospels existed in Anglo-Saxon with ecclesiastical approval, had not the "profanation" of the Scriptures been committed irrevocably? And in what sense was a vernacular Bible "unthinkable" in the mediaeval Church, if the Italians had one, the Spanish had one, the French had several, and the Germans even more?

Actually, as the historians frequently tell us, in its isolation from the Continent, Britain in the Middle Ages lagged somewhat behind the intellectual development of Europe. That is one reason why the first translation into what we would now

[5] *Ibid.*, p. 84.

call English was Wycliffe's Bible, and why the
early history of the English Bible is largely Protestant. After Wycliffe came printing, followed
shortly by the Reformation, then a series of English Bibles, most of them produced by bitter
enemies of the Catholic Church, none of them with
her approval. In fairness, however, it should be
added that the other Protestants, including the
civil authorities ruling in England, were as censori-
ous of most of these Protestant translations as
were the Catholics. Also, when the exiled Catholic
scholars resident in Douay and Rheims at last
brought out the first complete biblical translation
into English done with Catholic authorization
(the New Testament in 1582 and the Old Testament in 1609), it was refused entry into the England of the Reformation.

The favorite reason for the condemnation of
Bibles in those days was the trimming of notes and
comments appended to the biblical text by the
translators rather than the text itself. When the
Rheims editors pilloried the new religion in England so mercilessly in their preface and notes, they
left the Elizabethan government with little choice,
under the prevailing notions of censorship, but to
keep the Douay Bible out of the country if possible. In the same way, the Catholic Church had

little choice but to condemn translations which were merely vehicles for propaganda against Romish error, as so many of the English Bibles were. It was not a polite age, people felt very strongly about what they believed, and religious controversy was often bitter.

Occasionally there was question of deliberate tampering with the biblical text, though some Catholic apologists have exaggerated this factor in their eagerness to justify the Church's discipline. The classic instance always cited is of Martin Luther's insertion of the word *allein* into St. Paul's formula, "Justification is by faith." Now actually, to say that "justification is by faith only" is not to do treason to Paul's thought in its context, where he is speaking of the grace of initial justification which cannot be merited by any human work, since the necessary condition for merit is lacking. This is also Catholic teaching. But it must still be remembered that Paul had not actually said what Luther made him say, and to translate his words in this fashion in the midst of the Reformation controversy over the salutary nature of any good work whatsoever was to turn the Pauline text into a slogan for Protestantism. I do not believe that anyone today would deny that this was a mishandling of the Scripture. Tyndale acted in a more ambiguous way in his English New Testament of 1525, universally translating *episkopos* "overseer," *presbyteros* "elder," and *ekklesia* "congregation." It is true, the etymological sense of these words is quite what Tyndale made of them, and there is at least one modern Catholic version of the New Testament that translates them almost in the same way. But Tyndale was not interested in etymologies, but in denying that there was an historical continuity between Apostolic Christianity and the Catholic Church of the sixteenth century. He was, therefore, making religious propaganda in the guise of biblical translation, at a time when Catholics were insisting, and quite rightly, that the office as well as the name of the New Testament *episkopoi* and *presbyteroi* had been preserved in the bishops and priests of the Church.

Deliberate corruption of the text was, however, always the exception rather than the rule. No Catholic scholar today would care to defend all or most of Thomas Ward's charges in this regard in his *Errata of the Protestant Bible*. The Church has never felt any obligation to justify her disapproval of a translation on the plea that Protestants must invariably mistranslate, either wilfully or through ignorance. The decree against Wycliffe's Bible which we read above makes no claim that the version was a bad one. As a matter of fact, none of the copies of this Bible that are still in existence contains any distorted translation, and the fact that some of these copies were once owned by high Church prelates is proof that the translation itself was regarded as orthodox. Wycliffe's Bible was proscribed because it was unauthorized, and because it was used to further the Lollard heresy. The first action taken by the Church against any vernacular Bible of which we have record, the decree of Pope Innocent III in 1199, was taken for precisely the same reason, against a French translation used in the diocese of Metz by a secret lay society that was preaching ecclesiastical disobedience. Again the claim was not made that the translation was erroneous, but that it was tarred with the brush of its sponsors. That a version issues without ecclesiastical approval was and is the reason for its sequestration by the Catholic Church.

Few Protestants who read these pages will need to be told that their Catholic neighbors are perfectly free to read the Bible in their own tongue. They have seen, let us hope, Bibles in the homes of their Catholic friends, and if they have troubled to examine them, they have also seen that but for details the Bible used by Catholics is the same as the Bible with which, let us hope again, they are already familiar. On further inquiry they may have learned that during the past century the Popes have repeatedly directed long and thoughtful letters to the Catholic world, urging a more general and a more profitable reading and study of the Bible.

But they may have wondered whether this interest in the Catholic Church is not a post-Reformation development, a response to Protestant stimulus. Protestant writers sometimes ask whether a like interest is encouraged in "Catholic" countries where the Church has things its own way. As it happens, in countries like Spain, France, and Italy there are available more Catholic versions of the Bible, more and better commentaries, dictionaries, and other tools of biblical study, and more societies for the promotion of biblical learning than are possessed by Catholics in America, Britain, or any other country with a prevailing Protestant population. Whether there is more Bible reading would be hard to say. The habit of reading the Bible, sad to say, has diminished among both Catholics and Protestants in these days.

As far as Catholics are concerned, it is doubtless true to say that the Reformation, far from being a stimulus to the use of the Bible, was indirectly responsible for a lethargy from which they are only now recovering. Just as the first local condemnations of Bible translations by ecclesiastical authority rose from the Church's warfare against certain French heresies during the thirteenth century, the first world-wide legislation regulating the use of the Bible in the vernacular was part of the Counter Reformation against Protestantism in the sixteenth. This legislation in itself was actually not too severe. What it served to do, however, was offer a springboard to those eager souls with whom we are ever afflicted, who leap into every intellectual struggle with the bludgeon of reaction, anxious to prove themselves more Catholic than the Pope by translating a contemporary discipline into essential policy. For some while, an influential group of Spanish theologians helped this cause. It was taken up by other hands when theirs failed, and Pope Pius XII was still combatting the last of them in his encyclical letter *Divino afflante Spiritu* of 1943, in which he definitively placed the official Church on the side of positive biblical study.

The Reformers—Luther, Calvin, Zwingli, and the rest in Europe, Cranmer, Knox, Tyndale, and the rest in Britain—had differed among themselves concerning many of the fundamental assertions of Christianity, but they had been at one in professing themselves founded on the Bible, independent of any ecclesiastical interpretation. It was to be expected that in some minds the Bible should become so associated with Protestantism that abandoning it could be thought a badge of orthodoxy. This is the same sort of mind that nowadays can be readily enrolled against any legitimate social objective which its opponents can show has engaged the interest, or the pretence of interest, of "the Communists." It did not prevail in the laws of the Church, but it affected the administration of those laws because it affected a good number of Catholics.

At the Council of Trent, convened tragically late to cope with the problems that had too long plagued the Church, some of the assembled fathers were for banning vernacular Bibles entirely, simply because vernacular Bibles had been used to spread Protestantism. The majority, however, acted with the good sense that marks most of the deliberations of Trent. What was finally enacted is substantially the practice that is now observed, and which was already presupposed as early as the time of Wycliffe, that the licensing of vernacular versions should be the concern of the local bishop for his diocesans. The Council ordered an end to the anonymous publications of the Bible that had done the most to provoke anti-vernacular reactions, and, be it noted, it also directed certain positive steps to be taken towards providing critical editions of the Bible in the Latin and the original languages, with the ultimate aim of bringing about a wider and more informed use of the Scriptures.

Some only of Trent's directions were carried out, and these imperfectly. Nor was the Tridentine moderation always preserved during the difficult days that had come upon the Church. The regulation of Paul IV, in 1559, substituting the Holy See for the local bishop as the licensing authority for vernacular translations, was obviously not designed to make the use of the Bible easy for the ordinary Catholic. This regulation, repealed as too harsh by Paul's successor, was for a time restored under Sixtus V. It would therefore be folly to deny that for a while—even though it was a very short while in her lifetime—the Church did most definitely discourage the reading of the Bible in the vernacular.

When we have admitted this much, however, we should also try to understand this attitude, as the attitude of any period must be understood, in its historical perspective. We must realize how such measures were thought to be necessary by churchmen of that time, who were not evil men even though they were sometimes shortsighted and precipitate. It is easy for us today, knowing as we do that the mediaeval Christian unity they were desperately trying to preserve had already been irrevocably shattered, to see their errors. But certainly the speedy disintegration of Protestantism into its fissiparous units, with its by-products in the anarchism of peasants' wars and the nihilism of the Anabaptists, was not showing the Church many salutary results from the wide distribution of the vernacular Bible. Suppression was perhaps not the answer to the Church's problems, but it could have appeared to be even to liberal-minded men. At any rate, suppression was never adopted as a permanent policy.

The extraordinary revival of interest in the Bible in recent years in Catholic circles can be attributed as much to the fact that Catholics have at last shaken off the final vestiges of reaction to the Reformation as to any other cause. At least, this is largely true in "Catholic" countries, where Catholic biblical study is much more flourishing than it is in lands where Catholics live among a Protestant majority. A constant concern with apologetics, however needful this may be in itself, is not productive of advance and progress in history, in the Bible, in theology, or in any other science, for apologetics of its very nature tends to hammer away at elementary proofs, put as simply and unequivocally as possible. To the extent that Catholics have been able to set aside the Reformation controversy, not as a task completed, but as one in which every issue has by now been adequately covered, they have been able to devote themselves to a fresher appreciation of the treasures of their faith. One facet of this has been the rediscovery of the book of our origins, the Bible.

CHAPTER 2

The Rule of Faith

When in an introduction to another book[1] I
sketched the approach to the Bible which is the
subject of the foregoing chapter, several Protestant
reviewers, while sympathetic to the broader purposes I was trying to serve, took occasion to re-
mark on the "great pains" I was at to explain the
legislation of my Church, "a task that is not in
every instance always easy to uphold." Their reactions, I think, can best of all illustrate the difference that still exists between the thinking of
Catholics and Protestants in relation to the Bible.
For from the Protestant point of view, when all
is said and done, any restrictive action at all that
is taken by the Church in connection with Bible
reading and study can hardly be justified. This is
a point of view that follows from the most funda-

[1] *A Path Through Genesis* (New York and London: Sheed
& Ward, 1956).

mental assumption of the Reformation, which is still honored, by profession if not in practice, by modern Protestantism.

The great Reformers held that all truths necessary for salvation were to be found in the Scriptures and were to be found so plainly expressed that the ordinary devout reader could discover them for himself. They dwelt much on the sufficiency and perspicuity of the scriptures. Difficulties remained and perhaps would always remain, to exercise men's faith, but normally scripture was its own interpreter and light on its dark places could be derived from the texts whose meaning was clear. In exalting the scriptures over against Mediaeval Church tradition, the followers of the great Reformers assumed the perfection of the scriptures. The Bible was the source of guidance and enlightenment in every department of human life and thought. The Puritans tended to push the claim so far as to insist that no action in daily life could be regarded as righteous unless expressly warranted by Holy Writ. Whatsoever is not of faith is sin, and faith is not, save where there

is an appeal to the word of God, and the word
of God is the scripture.[2]

Such a position would be held today in Protestantism only by certain of the "fundamentalists,"
who are many in numbers but who count for little
in the intellectual life of the religion of the Reform.
To all others, historical criticism has long since
proved that the Bible does indeed need interpretation that it cannot give itself, and that it is not
alone an adequate guide in every department of
human life and thought. Yet even those Protestants who are most thoroughly aware of the historical nature of the Bible retain in their thoughts of
it something of the first Reformers' assumption of
the sufficiency and perspicuity of the Scriptures.
These lines, for example, appear in an excellent
little book written recently by Canon J. E. Fison:

The church formed the canon, or rule, or
standard, of New Testament scripture, so as
to subject herself to it, and in doing so made
clear the true relation between scripture and
tradition. The church was responsible for the
writing of the New Testament: every book

[2] H. G. Wood, article "Bible," in *The Encyclopaedia
Britannica* (14th ed.), Vol. 3, p. 500.

was written by a churchman. It was the liturgical, pastoral, and evangelistic needs of the
church which caused them to write as they
did and when they did, and it was those needs
that largely determined the choice of material
selected for their writings . . . The church
cannot, therefore, be separated from the
scriptures, but neither can it, if it is true to
its own original intention, exalt itself above
the scriptures. The formation of the canon
was designed to have precisely the opposite
effect.[3]

Now if this judgment is sound, that the Church
once subjected herself to the Scriptures—which
could only mean that the Church has submitted
her teaching to the independent evaluation of the
scriptural exegete—then it is obviously true that in
placing hedges about the use of Scripture the
Church has gone back on her own constitution and
violated a primitive trust. If the Church once decided that this miscellany which is the New Testament, a collection of primitive Christian doctrine,
ritual, pastoral exhortation and morality, history
and apocalyptic, should henceforth stand as a sign

---

[3] *The Faith of the Bible* (Harmondsworth: Penguin Books,
1957), p. 189.

by which she might be contradicted with impunity, then in restricting the reading of the Bible in the vernacular and in setting allowable limits of private interpretation the Church has indeed broken faith with the past. If the Church cannot "exalt itself above the scriptures," it obviously has no business making any laws that govern the Scriptures.

But what justification is there for any such view of the scriptural canon? I do not intend to write here in any polemical tone, but simply to set forth the attitude toward Scripture professed in the Catholic faith. I cannot do this, however, without noticing the shortcomings of an attitude that is, outwardly at least, so opposed to it. These shortcomings are, I think, quite evident.

For where do we read in any historical source that the early Church ever subjected herself to the Scriptures, or formed the canon so to do? How, in point of fact, could any such thing even have been possible, in view of the fact that every judgment and determination of policy made by the Church in her most formative years was perforce made independently of any scriptural canon? Probably the various New Testament writings were already being gathered together shortly after they were written, and it is possible that a collection of the Pauline epistles may have existed be-

fore the last New Testament writing was complete.
But the canon was long in forming.

At one time or another certain books of the
N.T. were not accepted—*e.g.*, *Hebrews*,
James, Jude, and especially *Revelation*. The
anti-Semite Marcion (about A.D. 140) vehe-
mently condemned the O.T. and much of
the New which he considered 'judaïzing'; he
appears to have been the first to force the
Church to fix a Canon. Tindale (like
Luther) printed *Hebrews, James, Jude* and
Revelation at the end of the N.T. as being of
lesser value. On the other hand, in early
Greek MSS. are to be found the *Epistle of
Barnabas,* the *Shepherd of Hermas,* two
Epistles of Clement to the Corinthians, and,
in one case, the *Psalms of Solomon.* The N.T.
Canon reached its final form during the
fourth century A.D.[4]

The fourth century is, in fact, rather an opti-
mistic summary of the case. Actually, almost as
much Christian history had passed by—and, be
it noted, history of far greater magnitude—by the

[4] Stanley Cook, *An Introduction to the Bible* (Harmondsworth: Penguin Books, 1945), pp. 36 f.

time the canon achieved its final form, as has passed by from the Reformation to the present. During that period had lived and died the greatest of the Church fathers, whose testimony to the faith of their times is appealed to not only by Catholics but by Protestants as well. During that period Church councils had met, decisions had been made that settled Christian questions for a thousand years, heresies had been repudiated, policies of far-reaching import had been undertaken, and, day in and day out, the Christian life had been led by hundreds of thousands and millions of Christians. All this, it is true, was not done without the guidance of Scripture, but it was certainly done without any definitive canon of Scripture. That Scripture was, or could have been, during these formative years the Church's written constitution is therefore evidently false on the face of it. Rather, it was quite the other way round. The Church was in this time determining which of her earliest writings merited inclusion in the Christian counterpart to the Old Testament inherited from the Jews; and one of the criteria of acceptability was that these writings should agree in doctrine with what was believed and taught in the Church.

We are not forced to conjecture about what was normative Christianity in these times. It was not a canon of Scripture that did not exist, but a Church authority that did exist. The first Christians "gave steadfast attention to the teaching of the apostles and to union, to the breaking of bread and to the prayers" (Acts 2,42). The Apostles themselves had now passed from this world, but it was not thought that their authority had passed with them; rather, that it had remained in the Church that preserved the teaching of the Apostles, even as it preserved union, the breaking of bread, and the prayers.

All of you, obey your bishop as Jesus Christ obeyed the Father, and obey the priesthood as you would the Apostles. Reverence the deacons also, as God commands. Apart from the bishop, let no one do anything of what pertains to the Church. The only true Eucharist is the one performed by the bishop or by him whom the bishop has appointed. Wherever the bishop is, there must be the congregation, just as wherever Jesus Christ is, there is the Catholic Church. Apart from the bishop, it is unlawful either to baptize or to celebrate an *agape,* but whatever he approves is pleasing to God. . . .

Such were the words of Ignatius, the bishop of Antioch, in his *Letter to the Smyrnans* (8, 1) about 107 A.D., as he was on his last journey to martyrdom. They are words, written when the memory of the Apostles was yet living among men who had known them in their youth, which offer little comfort to the view either that this early Church was in any doubt about its means of determining its convictions and actions, or that it was prepared to submit these to any judgment independent of the official Church. It was, in fact, only this assurance of a transmission of authority that made possible, slowly and by degrees, the Church's final determination of the canon of Scripture. About the middle of the fourth century, Cyril, the bishop of Jerusalem, was writing (*Catechesis* IV):

There are but four Gospels of the New Testament, for the rest are pseudepigrapha and harmful. The Manichees also wrote a *Gospel according to Thomas,* camouflaged with the appearance of being a Gospel, which corrupts the minds of the unwary. Accept also the *Acts* of the twelve Apostles, and besides these, the seven catholic epistles of James and Peter, John and Jude. Finally, as the seal placed on the whole and the last work of the disciples, accept the fourteen epistles of Paul. Everything else should be kept outside as secondary. And whatever is not read in the churches, do not read even privately, just as you have heard.

For one thing, St. Cyril's instruction shows that the canon was still in formation, for his list is narrower than the one that was finally adopted. But the important thing is what he tells us of the bases on which the canon was then being raised. (1) Firstly, orthodox doctrine was an essential. On this grounds the Manichean Gospel of Thomas was to be rejected. But obviously, the four Gospels which Cyril and the rest of the Church accepted could no more qualify their own orthodoxy than could the Gospel of Thomas. In view of the critical facilities of the time and the lack of scientific methodology, the Gospels were quite as ancient and as far removed from the Christians of the fourth century as they are from us today, if not more so. Normative Christianity itself, what was taught and believed in the Church, provided the attestation or orthodoxy. (2) Secondly, the apostolic origin of the Scriptures was a requisite. This

was never taken to mean that each writing of the
New Testament was actually the work of an
Apostle—from the very beginning the second and
third Gospels, and the Acts of the Apostles, were
attributed to authors who had never been Apostles
—but directly or indirectly each was considered
to be the product of an apostolic school. Here
again there was required a judgment that, for the
most part, could be supplied only on Christian
tradition. The Gospel of Mark, for example, was
held traditionally to reflect the apostolic catechesis
of St. Peter, a belief that modern critical studies
have supported. It was this tradition that ulti-
mately won the battle to include in the canon
certain doubtful books that have already been
mentioned. It was this tradition, too, that finally
ruled against others, though their teaching was
perfectly orthodox, such as the Epistle of Barnabas. (3) Finally, Cyril makes it quite clear that
the ecclesiastical use of a writing was necessary
in order that it should be regarded as canonical
Scripture.

It is generally admitted, I believe, that the canon
was eventually hammered out through a conflu-
ence of these criteria. They were not always taken
as having equal weight, and the argument for a
given writing might be much stronger in one rather

than another area. While a fairly unanimous
agreement had been reached on the New Testament by the fourth century, another two centuries
of debate remained before the Eastern and Western Churches had achieved harmony with regard
to some of the books of the Old Testament.
Throughout the entire process, one thing was always certain: that it was a decision for the Church
to make, on the basis of powers that were inherent
in the Church. Nowhere, either in the writings of
the contemporary fathers or in the decrees of the
ecclesiastical councils that made these decisions,
do we find any hint whatsoever that the definition
of the canon could make any difference in the rule
of Christian faith. That rule was to remain what
it had ever been, dependent on Scripture surely,
but equally dependent on the Church in which
the Scripture had its being. It is very true that nothing in the belief and profession of the Church
could be allowed to contradict the Scriptures—
it would be a monstrous thing, obviously, for an
organism which claimed to be the enduring pres-
ence of Jesus Christ and his Apostles to fly in the
face of the records of her origins from the same
Christ and the Apostles whose teaching she had
certified. But it was the Church—never a third
party, never a "disinterested witness"—that made

the decisions necessary to establish this continuity. A given article of Christian belief was held to be conformable with the sacred writings because the Christian Church had ever held that it was, and these decisions were not subject to the review of the independent exegete. Contrariwise, the exegete who separated himself from the Church to judge the Church in the name of the Bible was simply deemed to have removed himself from contact with any valid understanding of the Bible. Thus St. Jerome dismissed Tertullian's biblical argument against the virginity of Mary as of no account, since he had formulated it after his lapse into heresy. Never, either before or after the determination of the biblical canon, was scripture regarded as a rule of faith apart from the Church which had produced it.

The isolation of the Bible from the Church, the exaltation of the Bible over the Church—which in fact was the exaltation of the individual, however ignorant he might be, over a millennium and a half of Christian faith—was an inevitable conclusion which followed on the first principles of the early Reformers. This in turn led to the wholly unreal doctrine of the total perspicuity of the Scriptures, to which we shall return. It also led to a malformed idea of the sufficiency of the Scriptures.

In the book which I have already cited, Canon Fison states that

> within the canon of scripture, therefore, is to be found the full range and variety of understanding of the catholicity of Jesus Christ and his life and work, that is permissible within the Christian church. This is not to deny the obvious necessity for elaboration and development. History never stands still, and development is not arrested either by the death of the last original apostle or by the closing of the canon of apostolic writings. But it is to assert that only developments consonant with those apostolic writings can be regarded as legitimate expressions of apostolic Christianity. It is apostolicity which marks the permissible range of interpretation of the catholicity of Jesus Christ.[5]

This is an assertion that might well be made by a Catholic, though it might be phrased a bit differently. The substance of it is certainly admissible. But, I fancy, on grounds that the Reformers would hardly concede. Many of the early Church fathers also speak of the sufficiency of Scripture

[5] Fison, *op. cit.*, pp. 190 f.

as the rule of faith—yet never as having any validity apart from the Christian tradition of which it is a part. Once the Bible is conceived as standing outside the Church, as a source of doctrine it is valueless, whatever may be its many other ancient virtues.

Apart from Christian tradition, where is the antecedent of the Canon's "therefore" in his first line? He speaks, as we have spoken, of the criterion of apostolic origin, which we have seen could stand on no grounds other than Christian tradition. He speaks of a concept devised by Calvin, of the "autopistic" character of the Scriptures, that is, the quality of these writings to testify to their own divine origin. While there is something in this, of course, he must recognize that such a quality presupposes faith, it does not create it. There is no way to convince an unbeliever from the Bible itself that it is the word of God. And there is no way to convince either a believer or an unbeliever from the Bible itself that it is the whole word of God.

Apart from Christian tradition, there is no reason whatever to regard the Bible as anything other than what it obviously is, naturally speaking: a collection of disparate writings produced at various times by various authors, without consultation

of one another, dealing with only such matters as
were uppermost in the minds of the several writers,
totally ignoring others, occasioned in large part
by circumstances of casual occurrence. There was
no antecedent "grand design" for the whole Bible,
nor even for the whole New Testament, conceived
by any human author. Granting that we have in
the New Testament a gathering of writings dating
from apostolic times and directly or indirectly at-
tributable to apostolic authorship, what guarantee
is there that they represent "the full range and
variety of understanding" of apostolic Christianity, any more than the *Federalist* papers represent
the full range and variety of understanding of the
American Republic by its founding fathers? You
get a full range and variety of understanding
among a group of men only when they set out on
purpose to develop such a thing, not when a few
of their papers, written independently at different
times and places and in ignorance of one another,
are gathered together only at a much later date.

Now I hasten to agree that the New Testament
is not just a collection of ordinary writings, nor, indeed, is it an ordinary collection at all. It consists
of writings effected under divine inspiration and
collected with the guidance of divine providence.
Therefore, in obedience to this providence, I can

accept that this collection does indeed, at least in some fashion or other, run the full gamut of the apostolic understanding of Christianity. Many Catholics today would thus express their conception of the Bible. But faith alone can tell me this, and my willingness to accept the word of the early Church fathers who taught that it is so. Without this tradition, I have no reason to look on the Bible as anything but a casual aggregation of incomplete writings. And if I do follow Christian tradition so far, I am compelled to follow it still further, to see *how* the full range of the apostolic understanding of Christianity has been caught up in the New Testament. It is very obvious that it is not there in any systematic fashion, at least a great deal of it, but rather in adumbration, implicitly, latent in *obiter dicta,* indirectly expressed. The Christian tradition that found such utterance in the New Testament is necessary to my comprehension if what its writers had no intention or purpose of saying directly and clearly is to be made clear and direct to my mind.

John Henry Newman had reached this conclusion in 1838:

Yet while we admit, or rather maintain, that the Bible is the one standard of faith, there is no reason why we should suppose the overruling hand of God to go further than we are told it has gone. That He has overruled matters so far as to make the apparently casual writings of the Apostles a complete canon of saving faith, is no reason why He should have given them a systematic structure, or a didactic form, or a completeness in their subject-matter. So far as we have no positive proof that the Bible is more than at first sight it seems to be, so far the antecedent probability, which I have been insisting on, tells against its being more. Both the history of its composition and its internal structure are opposed to the notion of its being a complete depository of the Divine Will, unless the early Church says that it is. Now the early Church does not tell us this. It does not seem to have considered that a complete code of *morals,* or of Church *government,* or of *rites,* or of *discipline,* is in Scripture; and therefore so far the original improbability remains in force. Again, this antecedent improbability tells, even in the case of doctrines of faith, as far as this, viz., it reconciles us to the necessity of gaining them only *indirectly* from Scripture, for it is a near thing (if I may so speak) that

they are in Scripture at all; the wonder is, that
they are *all* there; humanly judging, they
would not be there but for divine interposi-
tion; and, therefore, since they are there by a
sort of accident, it is not strange that they are
there only in an implicit shape, and only indirectly producible thence. As in respect to
this earth, we do not find minerals or plants
arranged within it as in a cabinet—as we do
not find the materials for building laid out in
order, stone, timber, and iron—as metal is
found in ore, and timber on the tree,—so we
must not be surprised, but think it great gain,
if we find revealed doctrines scattered about
high and low in Scripture, in places expected
and unexpected. It could not be otherwise,
. . . supposing Scripture to be, what it is, the
work of various independent minds in various times and places, and under various circumstances.

Newman wrote this when he was still a few years
removed from his acceptance of Catholicism, when
he had come to see the unreality of the Protestant
position in which he had been educated, yet was
anxious to avoid what he then thought of as the

Roman position, that part of divine revelation only was to be found in Scripture, with other parts in oral tradition. After he had become a Catholic, he attached this footnote (in 1872) to the essay[6] from which I have just borrowed:

It may require explanation, why it was that the author, in this argument against Latitudinarianism, should so earnestly insist on the implicit teaching of Scripture, with history for its explicit interpreter, instead of boldly saying that, not Scripture, but history, is our informant in Christian doctrine. But he was hampered by his belief in the Protestant tenet that *all* revealed doctrine is in Scripture, and, since he could not maintain that it was on the surface of the inspired Word, he was forced upon the (not untrue, but unpractical) theory of the implicit sense, history developing it.

This is, perhaps, a better way of putting it, if only to avoid the impression that the "implicit" is more than we claim for it; it places the emphasis

[6] "Holy Scripture in its relation to the Catholic Creed." In the re-edition of Newman's works this is in *Essays and Sketches* I (New York and London: Longmans, Green & Co., 1948), pp. 201–330.

where it belongs, on tradition, of which Scripture
is one form. But Newman's original formulation
can be taken, too, as it stands. Catholic theology
has never resolved precisely the relation between
Scripture and tradition in the transmission of revealed truth. The Council of Trent defined that it
is "contained in the written books and in the un-
written traditions which were received from the
mouth of Christ by the Apostles, or by the Apostles
under the inspiration of the Holy Spirit"; but this
does not necessarily mean that it is distributed,
equally or unequally, between the two, but rather
that the two are complementary. The Scriptures
give written confirmation to tradition, and tradition is necessary to explicate the Scriptures.

At all events, what must be evident to anyone
who accepts "the obvious necessity for elaboration
and development" of which Canon Fison speaks,
is that this cannot be controlled by the "Bible
alone" formula of the first Reformers. What is a
legitimate development or elaboration, and what
is a betrayal of the spirit if not the letter of Scripture, are questions which Scripture itself cannot
always answer. For some "Bible Christians," an
episcopal government of the Church, or any insti-
tutional organization at all, an official such as a
Canon, the baptism of infants, and a hundred and

one other traditional Christian beliefs and practices held by Catholics and Protestants alike, are confidently to be proclaimed unbiblical and therefore pernicious. Protestants no more than Catholics can justify all of these things on the bare word of the Bible alone, for that word is not there. They must, as Catholics do, appeal to a traditional Christian understanding of the Scriptures, holding that as the earliest Christians found them not unscriptural, neither should anyone today find them unscriptural. While "the Bible alone," therefore, of the first Reformers remains a principle honored theoretically by Protestantism, in practice it is not at all workable. The only ones who can consistently abide by the principle are those who reject the whole idea of development and elaboration in the first place, and who believe themselves—all hundred varieties of them—to be following New Testament Christianity according to the exact letter of the Bible.

The modern interpretation of the New Testament has shown how wrong the Reformers were to attempt to divorce the Bible from tradition. The school of form-criticism has renewed our appreciation of the role of the first Christian community in shaping the form and content of the passages of the New Testament, and this has led to the insist-

ence of distinguished Protestant scholars on the
need to know well the faith of the primitive Church
before we can hope to make proper sense of what
the New Testament is saying.[7] Scientific exegesis
serves to prove that as the Bible did not develop
in a vacuum, but in a Church that antedated it, it
cannot be properly understood outside the tradition of the Church. Where Catholics really differ
from Protestants is in their refusal to pick and
choose amidst this tradition. If the early Church
was sound in regarding the baptism of infants as
scriptural, it was equally sound in naming Mary
the Mother of God. If the monarchical episcopate
is a legitimate elaboration of New Testament faith,
so are the seven sacraments.

The only ones, we repeat, who can rightly claim
to be the lineal descendants and true heirs of the
Reformers in their attitude to the Bible are our
fundamentalist brothers, and they can maintain
the "Bible alone" principle only by refusing to
come to terms with reality. It was this religion,
sometimes called "literalism" or "Bible Christianity," that Newman meant when he wrote, "to be
deep in history is to cease to be a Protestant." For
the fundamentalist, no early Christian history ex-

[7] For example, the monumental work of C. H. Dodd, *The
Interpretation of the Fourth Gospel* (Cambridge University
Press, 1955).

ists apart from the New Testament, or, if it exists at all, it is only to prove that Christianity from the very beginning had wholly and hopelessly departed from scriptural faith. The Christianity that is revealed in the writings of Clement of Rome and Ignatius of Antioch, when men yet lived who had known the Apostles, is obviously the key to the interpretation of much of the New Testament, even as any ancient document must, as a first principle, be set in its contemporary context. But the man who despises "man-made traditions" and throws himself upon "the Bible alone" can afford to ignore first principles; he substitutes for the historical Church that produced the New Testament a reconstruction of New Testament Christianity that has its being only in his inadequately informed imagination. In its crudest state fundamentalism has no better historical knowledge of the Bible than a book that tumbled down from heaven, printed in sonorous English and dedicated to the most high and mighty prince James; it approaches the book quite as the Moslem does his Koran. But even the relatively enlightened type of fundamentalism cannot save its "Bible alone" principle without the sacrifice of historical criticism, through ignorance or through design. This is not to poke fun at earnest and peaceable people who have discovered the essence of primitive Christianity to lie in the exclusion of organ music, or blood transfusions, or alcohol, or coffee and pepper, or buttons; it is to point out that these aberrations are directly traceable to the Reformers who rejected tradition as the interpreter of the Bible.

The "Bible alone" formula was a novelty able to develop only after Christianity had grown old, only after the canon of Scripture was of such ancient standing that the grounds for its acceptance could be forgotten and it could be torn from the history that had given it being, to exist henceforth without genealogy. It was adopted of necessity by the Reformers because from their standpoint the living tradition of the Church in which the Catholic viewed, and still views, the Bible had become deceitful. They had concluded, haltingly at first, then more boldly, that for a considerable time the Church had been in grievous error, not simply in questions of discipline which had initially provoked the Reform, but also in questions of doctrine. To the Catholic it was and is still incredible that the whole Church of Christ could err in any essential of Christian faith and moral teaching, however the conduct of its members might fall short of the mark laid down by the Master. When

the Reformers had decided that the teaching of the
Church was no longer a safe guide for belief, it
was inevitable that they should resolve upon the
all-sufficiency of the Bible.

We have argued that the modern criticism of
the Bible has proved conclusively that this principle cannot work. Within the early Reform itself,
indeed, the principle was speedily shown to be un-
workable, if anarchy was to be avoided. It was not
long before various "confessions" and "profes-
sions" and "articles" were appearing to crystallize
and standardize the concept of biblical faith possessed by the various Reform groups, setting up
new traditions that were to be normative for the
future. These replaced the General Councils of the
Church recognized by Catholics and traced by
them from the Council of Nicaea in A.D. 325 down
to the Council of the Vatican which adjourned in
1870. The major Protestant bodies, in holding to
these devices as the price of their ecclesiastical
unity, thus recognize the need of an external control to the Bible, though they continue to profess
its exclusive sufficiency. It is quite true, these con-
trols often go unenforced, and a body like the
Church of England can embrace the most rigid
Anglo-Catholic in one arm while holding within
the other an independent spirit like Bishop Barnes

of Birmingham, who died asking himself if he were a Christian. But it is also quite true that this liberty can be allowed only because the extreme dissidents are in the minority; the broad body of the Church does hold to its established tradition.

The corollary of the Bible's sufficiency in the minds of the Reformers was its perspicuity. This principle, too, of course had speedily to be modified in practice. Theoretically, the individual Christian judgment and not ecclesiastical tradition determined the meaning of Scripture. Texts like John 16, 13 were cited to prove that the Holy Spirit would enlighten the understanding and shield it from error. To these assurances the Church had always appealed in holding that the Spirit of God would protect the faith of the Church as such, not that the individual Christian was to be permitted to isolate himself from the Church—the climate understood in the New Testament as being vital to all the activity of the Spirit—with the expectation of finding divine guidance through Holy Writ. And, again, the early history of the Reform itself, quite apart from the more realistic view of the Bible which modern study has given us, demonstrated amply—unless, indeed, the Spirit of God was the breath of contradiction, affirming and denying the same proposition with equanimity, revealed alike in the cold logic of Geneva and the frenzy of Münster—that Scripture was not perspicuous to every Christian reader.

Among the hardy survivors still adhering to the Reformers' doctrine are the Bible Societies, who lay great emphasis on the fact that their broadcast dissemination of the Scriptures is done "without note or comment." Reprobation of these Societies by various Popes in past generations was sometimes taken, by these good people and by others, as further confirmation of the Catholic Church's determination to keep the Bible from the hands of the people. It is not that, but a repudiation of the philosophy of religion inherent in their procedure, which is rejected by Catholic Christianity and, as far as that goes, by not a little of Protestant Christianity as well.

No one would want to call in question the great good will of the Bible Societies, which have made the Scripture available to millions in literally hundreds of languages and dialects, at a nominal cost or free. This activity has been indirectly responsible for not insignificant progress in biblical science, through the problems of translation it has revealed, the discussion it has stimulated, and the valuable publications to which it has given rise. No one would want to suggest, in fact, that the

Bible Societies are doing more harm than good. But one may legitimately point out that the premise which underlies their activity has been proved unsound, not only in principle but empirically.

The text of the Bible is one thing for the conditioned student, and quite another thing for the person who does not possess the training to cope with its many difficulties. In her laws, the Catholic Church specifically allows the use of any honestly produced version of the Bible or edition of the original text, no matter under whose auspices these may have been published, to those who are engaged in the serious study of the Scriptures. She does not believe, however, that the Bible is a book to be given to the ordinary reader "without note or comment"; her commission is to preach the Gospel, not to suppose that it will preach itself.

The Bible is the work of men who were alien to our thought processes, who expressed themselves in idioms different from our own, who presupposed many things to which they barely allude, things of whose existence modern studies are only now making us aware. For example, to begin to understand the Book of Revelation (the Apocalypse of St. John) one needs a good background of Jewish apocalyptic, together with a fair knowledge of the history of the times. One needs these things, or one needs a good commentary on the Apocalypse. At the very least, one needs some guidance through its maze of lush oriental imagery and obscure symbolism, and some kind of introduction to its purposes. Is there anything notably sensible in putting the Apocalypse before the indiscriminate reader, however innocent he may be of the equipment to understand it, suggesting, in effect, that he is at liberty to draw what conclusions he will?

I choose the example of the Apocalypse deliberately, since several recent sects have formed practically their entire corpus of doctrine from an interpretation of it which every educated Protestant biblical student knows to be both preposterous and fantastic. It will not do simply to write off such people, who run into the millions, as inevitable casualties in the cause of propagating the Bible. No one who is respectful of the truth can be indifferent to such a spectacle, or want to encourage further spectacles of the kind. If religious faith has any objective validity at all, if Christian charity impels us to any sense of responsibility for the health of our neighbor's mind and soul as well as of his body, might we not at least think twice before we conclude that the spread of the Bible "without note or comment" is invariably an unmixed blessing?

Preachers have urged people to "read the Bible." People have tried, and have often been baffled. For though some passages are so clear that "he that runs may read," there are others (as in the Epistle to the Romans) so hard that to tell a beginner, "Read the Bible" is as unfair as if an elementary-school teacher were to say to his class, "Study Euclid." The Bible is not an easy book to read. Its gold is given sometimes in nuggets, as in the twenty-third psalm or the Sermon on the Mount; but more often it comes in ore to be dug, smelted, and refined. Books which give a brief introduction to each biblical book and place it in its approximate chronological order perform a necessary service and meet a claim long overdue, for they enable the reader to answer such questions as, "Who wrote this book, and why, and when, and where?"[8]

By all means, knowledge of the Scripture should be promoted, but there is more to this than simply scattering Bibles broadcast. The reading of the

[8] G. A. Buttrick, "The Study of the Bible," in *The Interpreter's Bible,* Vol. I, p. 165. Copyright 1952 by Pierce Smith. By permission of Abingdon Press.

Bible ought to be the desire of the man of faith, who ought also to use in his reading of it all the helps that ancient knowledge and modern scholarship can give him. Besides being a part of the world's literary heritage of which no literate person can afford to be ignorant, the Bible is for the man of faith a means of grace, a precious thing given by Almighty God, which must on no account be neglected. As such, it can be properly comprehended only by the man of faith, and to this end it was written for him by other men of faith. It is a book written to strengthen faith and to testify to the truth that makes us free, not to serve as an occasion of the error that makes us slaves forever. It was written to contribute to that unity of faith which, together with unity of love, the writers of the New Testament made the hallmark of Christianity. These purposes are well served when the Bible is used as it was first used, but they are not served at all when it is used as it has often been used since.

In summary, therefore, it is the difference between the Catholic's and the Protestant's rule of faith that accounts for much of the difference in their handling of the Bible. It explains not a little of what, to Protestant eyes, seems to be the Catholic's neglect of the Scriptures in his personal religious life. If the Bible is taken as a source book of faith, as Protestants still frequently take it, wherein each must make his personal decisions on the basis of his understanding, the Bible must inevitably loom large for whosoever values his religious life. But it is not so for the Catholic, who takes his faith from the Church. The Bible is not the whole of his religion, as it is for some Protestants.

This is not to condone Catholic neglect or ignorance of the Scriptures. One could, in fact, devoutly wish that Catholics were as eager to read and study the Bible as they are to proclaim that it is not the all-sufficient guide to salvation; for while it is not all-sufficient in truth, it is nevertheless a means of salvation divinely given. We are merely saying that what a Protestant may sometimes take as lack of respect for the Bible in a Catholic is not that at all, but a different hierarchy of values. The chapter-and-verse acquaintance with the Bible that a Catholic is not surprised to discover in a Protestant is hardly ever found the other way round. What the Protestant should understand, however, is that he has learned his Bible the way a Catholic learns his catechism. In Catholic eyes, it is far more important to know the catechism than to have the Bible by rote.

The Catholic rule of faith likewise accounts for ecclesiastical legislation that can scandalize the Protestant. The Church has never pretended— *pace* Canon Fison—to be subject to the Bible in any sense of the word that would appeal to a disinterested observer. She has, rather, insisted unequivocally that she is the custodian of the Bible and its interpreter, since she wrote the New Testament and accepted and defined the limits of the Old. She has never pretended that it was within the province of every Christian, whatever his qualifications, to interpret the Bible for himself, and therefore she has never held that the uncontrolled circulation of the Bible under every circumstance must of necessity be a good thing; therefore she has ever reserved to herself a jurisdiction over Scripture and a determination of its use. Since the Church has never maintained, as Luther is said to have done, that a ploughboy with the Bible in his hand stands equal with the Pope of Rome to settle religious questions, it is hardly reasonable to expect that she should have acted as though she did endorse such a proposition.

CHAPTER 3

The Bible in the Church

If the Catholic must refuse to the Bible, or rather, to the private use of the Bible, the normative function attributed to it by many Protestants, he does not and cannot thereby dispense with the Bible as a determinant of Christian faith. Though in a sense different from the Protestant one, the Bible is the Church's rule of faith, and the Church can no more dispense with the Bible than a nation can dispense with its laws and constitutions, though these are but dead scraps of paper when separated from the living body whose life is their life.

We are sometimes told, since in the Catholic view Scripture serves only to confirm the tradition of the Church, that it is at best superfluous in the life of the Church—it is tradition that always calls the tune, never the Scriptures. In a limited sense, this is true. The vast majority of Catholics believe as they do, not because they know that what they

believe can be verified in Scripture, but because
they believe that what has been taught them by
the Church has been revealed by God. Indeed, how
can we expect it to be otherwise? The vast majority
of men are not exegetes of Scripture, but faith is
intended for all. Even exegetes of Scripture have
been known to debate the meaning of a text. As a
matter of course, the average Catholic, like the
average Protestant, takes his belief from tradition.
The Scriptures may enter little or not at all into the
matter.

But this is to consider the question of belief only
from the standpoint of the believer, and the
Church is much more than the aggregate of those
who believe. To the Church has been committed
the active ministry of the word of God, in a tradition that is not static but living, and that therefore
must be fed from the springs of Christian thought
and the continuous re-examination of sources. The
contribution of the biblical scholar to this continuity is a vital one, whether the teaching Church
ever actually utilizes his researches or leaves them
to the private assimilation of her members. For
while *de facto* the Bible enters little, at least directly, into the forming of the average Christian's
faith, it is always the desired thing that it should
enter into the faith of as many as possible, and this

it can do, if only indirectly, through those who have the function in the Church of teaching others.

The relation of the Bible to the Church's teaching, as I have indicated, is poorly expressed by the formula "Scripture *and* tradition," as though the two had divided the deposit of revelation between them. The correct perspective is given in these words of Father William Leonard and Dom Bernard Orchard:

> We must not, however, imagine Scripture and Tradition to be like two distinct reservoirs receiving the waters of divine truth from distinct and separate springs. There is in a sense but one source of revealed truth, *viz.* divine Tradition, by which is meant the body of revealed truth handed down from the Apostles through the ages and contained in the doctrine, teaching and practice of the Catholic Church. Yet since a large and important part of that revelation was committed to writing both before and after the time of Christ the Church is accustomed to speak of two sources of revelation, oral Tradition and Scripture.[1]

[1] "The Place of the Bible in the Church," in *A Catholic Commentary on Holy Scripture* (New York and London: Thomas Nelson & Sons, 1952), p. 1.

I have further indicated that I share the view they go on to express with regard to the extent of the revelation contained in the Scriptures, agreeing with Newman that the natural probabilities are against it, but accepting it on the evidence of the early Church:

The question is sometimes asked whether all revealed truth may not be found at least obscurely in Scripture. It is impossible, however, to make an absolute affirmation in the terms of the above question; but, relatively speaking, so much is contained in the Bible that it is difficult to assert that certain particular truths of Christian faith and conduct are nowhere found in it. It is, for instance, said that the Bible nowhere teaches the distinction between mortal and venial sin. The distinction, it seems, is nowhere clearly enunciated, but it is hard to say that it cannot be gathered from the whole assemblage of passages where mention is made of great sins such as exclude from the kingdom of God and of other faults which do not seem to be regarded as seriously staining the honour of those who commit them.[2]

2 *Ibid.*, p. 2.

But whatever the extent of its contents, we have in the Bible the book of the Church's beginnings, fixed irrevocably in the writing of its contemporary world, but therefore all the more suited to the leisured thinking and rethinking of Christian men throughout the centuries. It is a heritage more precious than ever before, now that the methods of textual criticism have acquired such exactness that we can be quite certain of our reading of the original text in by far the greatest part of the Bible. It is more than a monument of our faith; it is the living word of God concerning which the Church can and does come to new and deeper conclusions, the fixed point around which her teaching continues to grow.

Occasionally Protestant biblical scholars publicly sympathize with their Catholic colleagues for lacking the freedom vital to productive research since they are held in any case to the interpretation of the Church. Perhaps Catholics themselves are partly to blame for this. They have so opposed the Catholic position with regard to the traditional understanding of the Bible to the Protestant position of the autonomy of private judgment as to seem to exclude the necessary role of private judgment in all scholarship. The false impression given is twofold: first, that the meaning of every biblical text has at some time or other been fixed for Catholics; and second, that adherence to "traditional" interpretation means simply saying the same things over and over again.

The fact is that the Catholic interpreter of the Bible does not consult the officials of the Church before, during, or after his exegetical labors. It is true that if he publishes his work, his book must have an *Imprimatur*, the license granted by a local bishop for the publication of material dealing professionally with religion. But the *Imprimatur* is a negative guarantee only, simply signifying the bishop's agreement that the author has not gone counter to any Catholic doctrine on faith and morals. It does not mean that what the author says is thereby approved by the bishop, only that he cannot officially reprobate it. The bishop may or may not concur in the author's conclusions; it is conceivable that he might be in total disagreement with them all, yet recognize that as they extend to areas over which the Church has formed no judgment, they cannot be rejected by him in his capacity of local doctor of the Church.

For as a matter of fact the Church in her long history has ruled decisively on the meaning of only a handful of scriptural texts, probably less than a dozen all together. Furthermore, as Pope Pius

XII pointed out in his encyclical letter on Sacred Scripture in 1943, the number of texts about whose meaning there is general consensus among the early Church fathers—a consensus which would establish the existence of a truly traditional interpretation—is no larger than the number of those in whose interpretation the Church has officially intervened. Finally, where Church teaching is involved is only in those texts which pertain to faith and morals, by far the smaller part of the Bible. There are numerous "biblical questions" which do not come directly into the purview of the Church's teaching. It remains, therefore, that the greater part of the Bible is a field "in the explanation of which the sagacity and ingenuity of Catholic interpreters can and should be freely exercised," as the Pope concluded.

The Catholic exegete does recognize canons guiding his research which are ignored by others, it is true. These, however, are a self-imposed discipline, to the extent that the Catholic by a free act of faith accepts the teaching of the Church as the context in which the Bible is to be understood. In other words, he recognizes that the results of his research cannot conflict with any revealed truth as taught by the Church, since he believes the teaching of the Church to be true.

The logic of this position should not be too difficult to grasp, and I do not believe that any Catholic interpreter feels that he is thereby at a disadvantage in comparison with the so-called independent critic. The independent critic also acknowledges inhibitions in his studies, though their motivation may be altogether different from the Catholic's. There is no such thing, strictly speaking, as a criticism that is independent in an unqualified and absolute sense, for such a thing is an impossibility. Every science begins with first principles which it does not and cannot of itself prove. The scientist who may think that he accepts nothing else, at least accepts the principle of contradiction, and would reject any conclusion, however attractive it might seem, that would involve him in one. The Catholic interpreter of the Scripture begins with the first principle that the Catholic faith is true.

The Catholic biblical student has many occasions to be grateful for his first principle, when he sees the periodical chaos into which exegesis and criticism can be thrown, either from the "right wing" of fundamentalism or the "left wing" of those who have cut themselves free of any restraint from the past. It is rarer for the same virtue to be perceived by a non-Catholic. Several years ago, however, a distinguished Protestant and one of America's most eminent biblical scholars observed in an address how Catholic thought had kept itself sane in a recent moment of critical upheaval—this time promoted by "the left"—because "Catholic scholars saw at once that these ideas could not possibly be correct."[3] As, in the event, sober study finally proved.

Parenthetically, in the interests of perfect honesty, the Catholic scholar must confess that at various times in history he has been harassed in the name of orthodoxy to the detriment of honest intellectual discovery, not by the Church but by some of the Catholics in the Church, which is an entirely different thing. It is very true that sometimes the loudest champions of "Catholic tradition" have proved to be quite ignorant of what that tradition really is, confusing it simply with reaction. In his encyclical letter of 1943, Pius XII put us on guard against "that indiscreet zeal which imagines that whatever is new ought for that very reason to be condemned." It is for this reason that we should understand very clearly what is this Catholic tradition about which we have said so much. By Catholics themselves it is not always

[3] W. F. Albright in *The Catholic Biblical Quarterly* 7 (1945), p. 27.

properly understood, and it is a term they use far too freely.

Though an interpretation of the Scripture might have become common among Catholics for centuries, even many centuries, it does not therefore become traditional in the sense that a later Catholic cannot contradict it. Catholic interpreters could err in the past just as they can err in the present, and often the interpreters of the past lacked adequate means to arrive at a sound evaluation of the Scriptures' meaning. That the patina which an interpretation acquires through age does not increase its truth is self-evident, but this is hard for some to grasp, particularly those who are reluctant to be put to the trouble of learning something new almost every year. As St. Cyprian once wrote in a letter, *Consuetudo sine veritate est vetustas erroris*—what is customary, if it falls short of the truth, is merely error in its old age. Modern Catholic interpreters have, as a matter of fact, overturned quite a few of these customary interpretations in the name of a better knowledge, and are, I trust, cheerfully prepared to see their own interpretations similarly overturned, should the broader knowledge of the future demand it. Their innovations—which are just as often a return to an older tradition that antedated the current, "cus-

tomary" one—have at times disturbed some of
their fellow Catholics (who of course, for the most
part, were honestly misinformed regarding Catholic tradition, not inflamed with the indiscreet zeal
of which the Pope spoke). Occurrences of this
kind would be rare if the desire the Pope expressed
in this same letter were to be realized, that the
fathers of the Church should be restudied and their
genuine teaching should become more generally
known. For the tradition that the Catholic interpreter is bound to respect is the *apostolic* tradition
reflected there, which has formed the true *teaching*
of the Catholic Church.

When it is a question of this truly apostolic tradition regarding the nature of what has been divinely
revealed, it is difficult to see how it can be thought
that the Catholic interpreter has somehow relin-
quished a right that free men ought to maintain,
when he refuses to contradict it. True, in the assertion of an opinion a man may be right against
the world, though it is always unlikely. This, however, is quite different. In holding that God has or
has not revealed a certain thing, no man can hold
this for himself alone; it inevitably involves his fel-
lows. For Christianity is not a private relation between an individual person and God but the revelation of a divine significance within various his-

torical events in which the whole of mankind has been caught up. When a man asserts, "Thus God spoke," he asserts it for every man, and when he denies that God said a thing, he denies it for all. It requires just as much religious assurance for a man to say, "God made no infallible Church," as for the Church to proclaim her infallibility. In rejecting Christian tradition, one must be prepared to claim for himself an authority he denies to the early Church.

A half century ago a brilliant Protestant exegete wrote, concerning the early Councils of the Church, that

the decisions in question were thus the outcome of a long evolution, every step in which was keenly debated by minds of great acumen and power, really far better equipped for such discussion than the average Anglo-American mind of today.[4]

This perspective of the early Church is the more usual one nowadays, in a generation that has learned to recognize Macaulay's quip about the

[4] William Sanday, *Outlines of the Life of Christ*, 2d ed. (New York: Scribners, 1908), p. 226.

homoiousion[5] controversy being a debate over a letter of the alphabet for the ignorant superficiality that it was. Something of the same violence is done to our sense of decorum, however, when without taking much more thought than is necessary to say the words, anyone who has convinced himself that he can read can feel free as a matter of course to scoff at "the unbiblical doctrine of mariolatry," as though the fathers of Ephesus who painfully formulated *theotokos* had been bumpkins unlettered in the Bible. Quite aside from doctrinal considerations, the humility that is required in any honest intellectual quest demands that we know of what stuff Christian tradition has been hewn.

But while Christian tradition is a guide to the Catholic interpreter, the road that he travels with it is really a two-way street. Tradition itself is in turn dependent on the Catholic interpreter: the Church looks to him in the very serious matter of the development of Christian doctrine. It is evident even to the casual reader of the New Testament that within the compass of the few years over which it was composed, the Church had become more aware, and more profoundly aware, of her

[5] *Homoiousion* ("of like substance") was the key-word of Semi-Arianism, which held that the Son was like the Father in substance but not identically one with him in substance or nature.

own significance and of the meaning of many of Christ's words. Such a development can be clearly seen in the distinctive personality of a writer like St. Paul, whose theology has been indelibly written into primitive Christianity. The process that we see in the New Testament did not, of course, stop with it. The teachings of Christ that inspired its writers still live to inspire us, and the writings that they also produced continue to evoke fresh thought in the minds of Christian men. It is the duty of the Catholic exegete, consciously working within the tradition of the Church, to contribute to the clarification and development of this tradition by his research into its origins as expressed in the Scriptures. If this contribution is to have any value, it must be effected through the use of every advantage which modern research has gained for us. "This true freedom of the sons of God," as Pope Pius XII wrote, "loyally maintaining the doctrine of the Church, and at the same time gratefully accepting as a gift of God, and exploiting, every contribution that secular knowledge may afford, must be vindicated and upheld by the zeal of all, for it is the condition and source of any real success, of any solid progress in Catholic science."

The Popes and General Councils of the Church do not make Catholic doctrine; they rather act as

the arbiters and evaluators of the examination and
probing that have gone on through the years into
the progress of the Christian knowledge of revealed truth. Catholics believe that the solemn
judgments which they reach in this area are certain, and protected from error by Almighty God.
But they do not believe that this comes about by
magic or by any miraculous intervention. The process is, instead, part of the order of divine providence, which means that the judgment occurs as
the climax to the perfectly normal working of
human minds, instructed it is true by God's grace,
but employing the same reason and tools of study
that they share with other men. By these means our
knowledge of Christian truths is broader than that
of the first Christians, though the truths are the
same. The unity of truth also requires that our
broadened knowledge be consistent with that
which stands at our origins. The labor and responsibility with which the interpreter of the Scriptures in the Catholic Church is consequently
charged are obvious.

However, the concern of the Church with the
Bible is not confined to it as a source of revelation.
It is owing in part to the influence of primitive
Protestantism that there is still a widespread con-
fusion of inspiration with revelation, whereas the

two are really distinct things. The Bible contains revelation, it is the medium by which revelation is made known, but it is not revelation itself. The Bible, all of it, on the other hand, is a work of inspiration, and it is as such, with all that this implies, that it has been given to the Church by God.

By "inspiration" we mean the factor in the composition of Scripture which distinguishes it from all other literature. In inspiration, God acts upon the mind of the human author in such a way that with the free exercise of his own faculties he writes what God intends him to write, or (as is the case in parts of the Bible), composes and assembles previous writings in the way God intends, to the end that the product may be called God's word as well as that of the inspired writer. The purposes God had in inspiration are various, and are admirably summed up in 2 Timothy 3, 16–17: "All Scripture is inspired by God and (or, All Scripture, inspired by God, is) profitable for teaching, for reproof, for correction, and for training in righteousness, that the man of God may be perfect, equipped for every good work." These words also tell us for whom inspiration was intended. The communication of revealed doctrine is only one of its purposes, and an occasional one.

In the inspired history of the Bible we are afforded the opportunity of learning from the actions of those who have gone before us, at the beginning of the story whose end is not yet—from their triumphs and their mistakes—the lessons which divine providence would have us learn to our profit today. We are asked to see what the writers of both the Old and New Testaments believed in every fiber of their souls: that all human history is the working out of a grand design—not, to be sure, one in which God has always had it his own way, in the monotony of a fatalism granting no scope to the wild and often irrational freedom of the human will, but a design in which providence, and not unreason, rules; in which every human act is known to be fraught with consequences for the future even as it proceeds from a man who has been shaped by the past. Perhaps especially in times like ours, when human words and deeds often serve no other purpose than to fill a void, when we are forever being urged to the pursuit of leisure, which means time set aside not to be used, we could gain much from the biblical conception of life. For the Bible permits us to see how full of meaning and consequence life and action can be, in that on certain determined events occurring in the definable moments of history have swung the destiny and salvation of all mankind.

In both the Old and New Testaments we are given the example of godly men and women which can teach us and train us in righteousness, as well as the example of ungodly men and women which can reprove and correct us. In the history and laws of the Old Covenant we can rediscover, even as it was first experienced, the condescension of the God who did a greater work than creation, who gently led a people by the hand from the most elementary things to an awareness of the moral will that governs the universe, with consequences that no man today can escape even if he would. We see men coping with problems that we must face, using the principles that we must use. We hear the thunder of words that are as applicable today as they were in the Israel of Amos or the Judah of Jeremiah. In both Testaments we are taught admirable ways to pray and to attend on God's mercy.

In the use of the Bible for prayer, the Church itself has always given its members the best possible example. The Psalms which came to the Church with a liturgical background from the temple and synagogue entered immediately into the Christian liturgy. The perennial attraction of the Psalms has been proof against every change of time and nation; their appeal has been truly catholic. Several years ago a Catholic organization dedi-

cated to the circulation of pamphlet literature
through paid advertisements in the press throughout the United States and Canada offered in suc-
cession free copies of the Gospels and the Psalms
to anyone who would take the trouble to write
for them. Both Gospels and Psalms were distributed in the thousands, but the advertisers were
mildly surprised to note that the ratio of requests
was several times to one in favor of the Psalms.
This, however, was only a latter-day echo of the
decision made long ago by the Catholic Church,
which has always constituted her public prayer
principally from the Psalms. In a normal week
every priest and member of a religious order which
has the "obligation of choir" will have recited the
entire Psalter once. He will also have read various
continuous passages from the Old or New Testament, including readings from the Gospels and
Epistles in the Mass of each day, and he will have
made countless allusions to practically all the
books of the Bible in the mosaic of scriptural
verses from which the Church's prayer has been
fashioned.

Today every encouragement is extended to the
Catholic to imitate the practice of his Church and
make the Bible as much his everyday literature as
it obviously once was for Christians. Time was

when the disuse of the Bible as reading could be
justified easily enough because of the archaic and
often incomprehensible English in which one was
expected to read it, as well as the lack of necessary
helps in the way of commentaries, atlases, con-
cordances and the like. Now all that has been
changed, or at least is well on the way to complete
change. It is now largely up to the reader to take
the initiative in providing the need which will call
forth a better supply of biblical materials. There
is every reason to hope, now that the voluntary
illiteracy of our mechanized society shows signs
at last of receding from its high-water mark, that
the Bible may be read again as soon as Shake-
speare is. Scholars of late have been agreeably
surprised to find that their studies of the so-called
Dead Sea Scrolls are being followed, if only re-
motely, by a wide—and an antecedently unlikely
—public. In recent months a respected biblical
archaeologist published his discoveries at Old
Testament Gibeon in a "slick" weekly magazine
whose pages have usually been by preference innocent of anything more complicated and unpre-
dictable than summer fiction. These are encourag-
ing signs.

When all is said and done, all the scholarly work
devoted to the Bible, apart from the personal

satisfaction it gives the few who are engaged in
it, is in large measure motivated by the desire "that
the man of God may be perfect, equipped for every
good work." Piety without roots in knowledge is
illusory, like the sterile mysticism of the East. The
critical study of the Bible is, therefore, absolutely
necessary if our biblical faith and our historical
religion are not to degenerate into sentiment and
nominalism. By the distribution of gifts with which
the Holy Spirit has endowed the Church, it is the
duty of the scholars to make the results of their
studies available, that they may accrue to the good
of the whole Church. It is the duty of those whose
office it is to instruct others in the Church to make
use of the findings of the scholars. It is the duty
of all of us to assimilate this study into a personal
appreciation of the Bible, and the pity is that we
do not do enough of it. Again the Church offers
us her own example, in contributing financially as
well as with the labor of some of her best biblical
scholars to the purchase and elucidation of such
documents as the Dead Sea Scrolls, for the sake
of the bearing they will have on the understanding
of the Bible that she has made so much a part of
her prayer and liturgy.

We have been taught, and it is true, that the
essential thing is to be doers of the word, not hear-

ers only. We cannot fail to do better, however, the
more we hear the word, reading it prayerfully and
wisely, asking the grace of understanding. It was
to this end that the Bible was inspired, and to this
end that it has been preserved for us. We can, if
we will, by its use become perfect men, equipped
for every good work. The devout reader discovers
for himself that the Bible, which begins "in the
beginning," ends with "the grace of the Lord
Jesus." That we might obtain this grace, our Lord
has left us his Church, and within his Church the
Sacred Scriptures.

14·101